How to boost productivity:

Proven strategies for peak performance at your workplace

James Dewitt

Table of Content

Chapter 1

Understanding productivity and its importance

The concept of "Productivity" is a popular issue today.

Productivity is for many of us an unquestionable good and a clear objective for both ourselves and the companies where we work.

Our feeling of productivity might appear to be a direct indicator of our level of success in life, and it can seem like a badge of pride. However, although everyone is talking about it, we don't always agree on what productivity really means.

The reality is that productivity is not only about crossing things off our to-do lists. Although it helps with corporate productivity, personal productivity has a completely distinct definition from business productivity.

Things might get complicated if you and your supervisor have conflicting ideas about what constitutes effective work. And ineffective.

In this chapter, we'll look at what productivity is, how it's been defined, how it affects you and your business, and how to increase productivity.

What is productivity?

The definition of productivity given by the Bureau of Labor Statistics is "a measure of economic performance that compares the number of goods and services produced (output) with the number of inputs used to produce those goods and services."

When individuals consider "being productive," they often consider what they are individually doing. That means crossing items off their "to-do" lists for many individuals. Your level of personal productivity demonstrates how well you do activities. However, not every assignment is made equal.

Various viewpoints on productivity

On a macro level, politicians, economists, and commentators discuss it. Managers and business executives are concerned about how their teams and staff will function in a hybrid environment. And the majority of us, personally, rate whether we "felt" particularly productive on a certain day.

These examples all contain various conceptions of production. Here are a few illustrations of various viewpoints on productivity.

Personal Effectiveness

In various situations, productivity may imply different things, particularly with the development of information labor and automation. Personal productivity is the consistency and effectiveness with which a person completes work or achieves objectives.

Knowing the various levels of productivity may make it easier for you to understand how your job productivity impacts that of your company and perhaps even how both connect to the productivity of your nation.

Nation-wide output

Productivity is a measure of a nation's ability to convert labor and resources (the input) into products and services (the output, or gross domestic product [GDP]). It is a broad indicator of economic development concerning other events occurring in the macroenvironment and reflects changes in policy and technology.

This may lead to the citizens of that nation having a greater level of life.

Business efficiency

Productivity evaluates a company's ability to make money from resources, labor, and inputs. In business, productivity is often defined as revenue divided by labor hours. A company's overall productivity level may not provide business executives with any practical information, but it might show them how they stand up to competitors or other industry leaders.

Organizational effectiveness

Our efforts, which could produce results or provide value in a different period, might appear far away from corporate productivity, which measures income concerning employee work hours in a quarter.

What does workplace productivity mean?

The contribution that each team makes to the overall success of the company is known as workplace productivity. To better understand how an organization may improve its processes, it monitors the output of people or teams.

What makes productivity crucial?

A key component of a successful company strategy is encouraging staff productivity which leads to business results. Additionally, it benefits the workforce.

Productivity increase is an indicator of a company's health and expansion for enterprises. A successful company may grow, adding new services and even cutting pricing.
Productivity is crucial for workers because it keeps them moving toward their maximum

potential. Being productive enables us to successfully balance our obligations to our jobs, homes, interests, and families.

How to evaluate the output

Personal productivity, whether at work or in life, may be challenging to quantify, particularly now that many individuals don't do repetitive jobs. It used to be much simpler to assess productivity by how many widgets a person could produce each hour.

In the era of knowledge labor, there is considerable debate about the subject of personal productivity. Innovative thinking and top-notch customer service are not easily reduced to an efficiency statistic. However, it's helpful to consider what productivity means for your particular profession and line of work. Then, whatever the statistic, strive to create the circumstances for improvement:

What is the right technique to evaluate worth or quality?

What is the appropriate amount measured?

What inputs do we want to utilize the most effectively?

The most important output to consider for both your teams and yourself is value. Productivity is calculated as (value of work) / (worker time and effort).

Although defining value may seem difficult, you may start by considering the results. When anything aids in the achievement of your intended results, it is useful to you (or to a business). Not every item on your to-do list offers the same benefits to you or others as others do.

This alters the way we think about productivity by including both the effectiveness with which an activity adds value and the efficiency with which we carry it out. The value of work in an organization is determined by how well it corresponds with organizational goals, how well it is performed, and how effectively it is completed.

The advantages of higher productivity

Being more productive is a common aim, but many individuals find it difficult to achieve.

Only 21% of office employees in the UK claim to be productive during the day, and an 8-hour workday typically only has 2 hours and 53 minutes of genuine working time.

Naturally, productivity issues faced by workers eventually show up in the production of the business as a whole.

Efficiency gain: By becoming more individually productive, individuals can work more effectively, perform errands more quickly, and have more spare time.

Enhanced workplace well-being Employees that are productive can better manage their time and feel more in control of their surroundings. When they are productive, some individuals could even love their jobs more, and they are also probably less anxious.

Enhancing both personal and business performance: Performance and production are traditionally linked. Each person's performance and productivity contribute to the success of the company, which results in reduced pricing, more profitability, and maybe increased compensation for workers.

Improved scalability: A company with high productivity levels makes better use of its resources and is prepared for development and expansion.

Describe some instances of productivity.

Getting the greatest output (or profit) from the input is the determining factor in both personal and commercial productivity. For enterprises, input may refer to expenses for capital, supplies, or labor. For humans, input often entails devotion, time, and effort.

Being inspired and motivated helps you be more productive. Employee motivation is a vital component of labor productivity.

Both personally and organizationally, there are various approaches to boost motivation and productivity.

When it comes to personal productivity, various methods may help you get more done each day without sacrificing quality. Popular examples include:

- dividing up larger jobs into smaller ones

- Using the Pomodoro Technique, which involves working in bursts of 25 minutes,
- establishing a calming morning routine
- Organizing your to-do list by priority to concentrate on the most important things
- Businesses may utilize gamification to inspire workers and raise engagement levels.

Microsoft reported a 10% improvement in contact center efficiency when they gamified their sales procedures. Additionally, 78% of their agents said they felt inspired and emboldened to work harder.

A strong corporate culture and an understanding of what inspires your staff may eventually boost performance, productivity, and profitability.

How is productivity achieved?

The majority of us are aware of the positive effects personal productivity has on our lives, but what about business or societal productivity?

When you're productive, getting what you want or producing something of high quality requires less time, effort, and mental exertion.

You are more productive when the outcome (getting what you want) is the same but the input (time, effort, and resources) required to get it is lower.

The same is true for companies.

Businesses are considered more productive when they generate more of a given output (goods and services) with fewer inputs (labor, capital, and materials).

Of course, it might be challenging to measure the results of our efforts in today's industry. (This is why so many people automatically use a checklist; it's simple to quantify "done" or "not done," even if it has nothing to do with value.) Value is given as a standard unit of product less often and less and less, making it difficult for people or enterprises to compare production.

However, you may compare the amount of work, time, and resources used to achieve a similar output of sales or income at the company level, taken as a whole.

Businesses calculate productivity by dividing the total income (or net sales) for a given time (the output) by the total number of labor hours provided by employees during that same period (the input). The labor productivity formula is what it is called.

What factors influence worker productivity?

A productive work atmosphere requires a lot of effort to create. Here are some of the most prevalent elements that businesses have improved to engage and inspire their staff to adopt a productive work culture.

1. Environment at work

The health and productivity of an individual are significantly impacted by their work environment. It consists of a variety of components, including leadership, management styles, corporate values, company culture, communication methods, and workplace trust. Spending money to make improvements in each of these areas reduces the likelihood of a hazardous workplace and increases output.

2. Growth Possibilities

Opportunities for professional development and career progression are motivating factors for many people. They like challenges, intriguing work, feeling that their efforts are recognized, and receiving compensation for their contributions. Try laying out your professional advancement routes to help teams get momentum and produce more.

3. Possibilities for socializing

Not everyone wants a daily job in an office. Some choose not to take part in group activities. However, it's crucial to provide chances for workers to interact, whether in person or electronically. Socialization fosters communication between teams, fosters cooperation, fosters innovation and builds trust. Team-building exercises may be social or professional.

4. Peer and manager feedback

In firms with positive feedback cultures, workers flourish. A recent poll found that 72% of workers believe that recognition is the factor that has the greatest influence on employee engagement. This does not imply that every criticism must be positive. However, making sure there are frequent check-ins with staff members and allowing them to provide feedback will assist boost productivity.

5. Psychiatric security

Productivity at work is closely correlated with psychological safety. Higher belonging is positively associated with sharper attention, better planning, and achievement of goals. These advantages provide a compelling justification for creating a psychologically safe workplace that makes use of communication, openness, and empathy.

6. Using resources and systems

The improvement of their digital employee experience is a key component in creating a more productive workforce. Giving people the resources they need to do their tasks effectively falls under this category. They may be utilized for transactional purposes, like sales enablement tools, or to maximize soft skills, like project management and communication tools.

In addition, many teams perform better when they have some kind of structure. Therefore, it is crucial to have systems and procedures in place for people to perform at their highest level.

7. Certain expectations

Teams may save a tremendous amount of time by establishing and expressing expectations upfront. Spending this effort upfront often reduces the time necessary for revisions or even redoing certain work.

Chapter 2

Identifying common productivity challenges

Have you ever noticed that some work days pass by quickly while others seem to drag on forever? Time is not the only factor; productivity also has a big impact on how we feel about our workdays. We get a feeling of success and contentment when production is high. But when we struggle to accomplish tasks, the day might seem like an endless grind. Unfortunately, office productivity issues are all too often.

Numerous variables, like poor time management, interruptions, and a lack of enthusiasm, may reduce productivity and leave us feeling irritated and overburdened. The good news is that these obstacles may be overcome with the appropriate tactics and mentality.

Every effective workplace is built on productivity, which is also essential to achieving organizational objectives. Unfortunately, several typical productivity issues often prevent workers from doing their best work. Individual barriers to productivity include things like distractions, a lack of enthusiasm, and ineffective time management techniques.

Any organization's success depends on its ability to overcome these obstacles. For instance, giving staff members training in time management and motivational strategies might increase productivity. Policies that discourage distractions and promote attention may also have a good effect.

For every company to succeed, productivity problems in the workplace must be resolved. Organizations may increase productivity, accomplish their objectives, and foster a great workplace culture by recognizing and resolving these difficulties.

We'll examine some of the most typical productivity issues at work in this chapter and provide helpful advice for resolving them. Therefore, we have you covered whether you're an individual trying to increase your productivity or a manager aiming to enhance team performance. Let's take on those productivity obstacles head-on!

1. Communication Issues

To understand their roles, responsibilities, duties, and objectives, employees should be transparent with their coworkers. Similarly, the manager must successfully interact with their team members while handling any comments, issues, projects, or other matters. Employees look to their bosses for guidance and advancement.

Employee uncertainty about what to accomplish and how to do it may have a detrimental effect on an organization's productivity. Instead of concentrating on the assignment, they may spend a lot of time attempting to comprehend the expectations.

Miscommunication may result in misconceptions, holdups, and errors that impede development. Effective communication methods must be established to overcome this obstacle. Promoting open communication among team members may assist create a healthy work atmosphere, which is one approach to this.

Software and solutions for project management may also facilitate team member coordination by streamlining communication and cooperation. Check-ins with the team regularly might assist address any concerns or problems that are impeding production. Teams may collaborate more effectively to achieve common objectives by emphasizing clear and succinct communication.

2. Procrastination

A common issue that might result in less productivity at work is procrastination. Many individuals put off critical chores till the very last minute, and when the deadline is approaching, they rush to do it and could neglect some crucial procedures, lowering the quality of their work. Delaying activities results in a backlog of work that has to be finished, which raises tension and anxiety levels.

Procrastination may also cause a lack of desire and attention, which can result in subpar work and missed deadlines. Determine the underlying reason for procrastination to create an effective approach for overcoming it.

Setting realistic deadlines and segmenting activities into smaller, more manageable chunks are two effective ways to fight procrastination. In addition, combating procrastination may be aided by holding oneself responsible for progress and asking for assistance from colleagues or bosses.

3. Multitasking

To do jobs more quickly, it is a good idea to concentrate on many things at once, albeit this might reduce productivity. When you attempt to multitask, you divide your concentration and attention, which makes it challenging to do activities to the best of your abilities and reduces productivity.

Prioritizing activities according to their relevance and urgency is crucial to overcoming the multitasking productivity difficulty. Start with the most important job first, then work completely on it until it is finished, then move on to the next. To retain attention and avoid multitasking completely, it may also be helpful to remove any potential distractions, such as by turning off alerts or locating a quiet office.

4. Not Being Motivated

Anyone may find it difficult to stay motivated, and this is true in the job as well. However, a lack of motivation may result in poor morale and lower production, which can be detrimental to a business's growth. Employees may lack motivation for a variety of reasons, such as feeling unappreciated or being bored.

Companies could think about providing incentives and prizes for achieving objectives or finishing work to address the issue of low motivation. Employee engagement and burnout may both be prevented by encouraging breaks and self-care. Giving workers chances for professional development and progress may do a lot to keep them engaged and motivated in their job.

5. Digital Distractions

Social media and the development of technology have made it simple to get sidetracked at work. Unfortunately, one of the biggest problems workers have at work is electronic distractions, which lower productivity and raise stress levels. Focus and creativity at work may be increased by encouraging people to take breaks from technology and participate in other activities.

To reduce workplace distractions, for instance, create limits at work and schedule time to check emails and social media. Additionally, distractions may be decreased by using productivity tools like internet filters or applications that restrict phone use while at work. Additionally, establishing a tech-free area in the office may aid in minimizing distractions and enhancing overall efficiency.

6. Inadequate time management

The ability to manage your time well is essential for continuing to be productive at work. Unfortunately, many people have trouble efficiently managing their time, setting priorities, and juggling their professional and personal life. Missed deadlines, lost productivity, and increased stress may result from poor time management.

To overcome this difficulty, clearly defining objectives and priorities is necessary. Distractions should be avoided and a timetable should be made. Effective time management may also be aided by calendars, to-do lists, and time-tracking applications. Procrastination may be defeated and staying on schedule is made easier by breaking activities down into smaller, more manageable stages.

Another well-liked method is the Pomodoro technique, which encourages people to work in short bursts with pauses to increase concentration and productivity. Regular breaks and self-care routines may also aid workers in recharging and preventing burnout in addition to these measures. Encouragement of workers to participate in extracurricular activities may help enhance attention and eventually increase productivity.

Employers may increase employee productivity and engagement by emphasizing time management skills that work and encouraging self-care behaviors.

7. Burnout and stress

Stress and burnout are frequent productivity issues that may adversely affect a person's effectiveness at work and overall well-being. Chronic stress may cause fatigue, a lack of enthusiasm, and even physical health issues. On the other side, burnout is characterized by cynicism, disengagement from one's job, and diminished effectiveness.

For increased productivity and general well-being at work, taking frequent breaks and practicing self-care is crucial. Encouragement of workers to take brief breaks and practice yoga, stretching, or mindfulness techniques, for instance, may aid in their ability to concentrate and get their energy back. Additionally, employers might provide their staff members access to a specific relaxing room or nutritious food during their break. Promoting a culture of self-care may promote employee engagement and happiness, which will eventually boost productivity.

Additionally, showing workers that their employers care about their well-being by encouraging them to prioritize self-care may enhance morale and prevent burnout.

Conclusion

It might be difficult to overcome the productivity obstacles at work, but they are not insurmountable. You may foster a more successful and happy work environment by identifying and resolving the sources of these problems. It's critical to keep in mind that productivity requires not just working harder and longer hours, but also working smarter.

You must prioritize projects, properly manage your time, use good communication techniques, and foster a healthy work atmosphere if you want to overcome these difficulties. Invest in staff training and development opportunities as well to enhance their abilities. Processes may be streamlined and distractions can be decreased with the use of technology. You may overcome productivity obstacles at work and succeed by paying attention to these suggestions.

Chapter 3

Setting meaningful goals to achieve success

Setting objectives at work requires striking a delicate balance. Your workplace objectives must, on the one hand, support the corporate purpose. They must, however, belong to you. Otherwise, making goals is merely a mindless, box-ticking process.

The fact that some businesses (and managers) are better than others at assisting their workers in setting and achieving professional objectives adds another layer of complexity. The good news is that there are things you can do to get some value out of the yearly goal-setting session, even if you work for someone who views it as a necessary evil.

You have a fantastic chance to utilize the talk to advance your career if your boss appreciates the value of goal alignment and the importance of creating and attaining career objectives.

Before creating objectives at work and completing your goal sheet, consider the following ten considerations.

1. Identify the structure of your team.
First things first: to define office objectives that will increase your team's productivity and benefit the rest of the company, you must first understand the roles and connections within your team. Practically speaking, every team functions as both a provider of assistance and a unit that receives it. If the mapping is done correctly, you will be able to pinpoint precise, quantifiable improvements you can make to make projects and processes operate more efficiently.

2. Speak to your manager.

What can you do to facilitate their work and enhance their image?

Despite what your job title may indicate, the main focus of your duties is to make your manager's life simpler. Consider it a chance to help someone else. Your job objectives may be defined by having an open dialogue with your manager and often asking them questions.

3. Have a strategy for the things you can influence and concentrate on them.

There are things you can manage and ones that you have no control over for any employment objective. Make sure you understand the difference and have a strategy in place in case the uncontrollable circumstances don't pan out.

Consider that you are a manager in a hospital's accounting division. Let's imagine you decided to shave two business days off the month-end closing schedule. Success will rely on the expertise and teamwork of your accounting department—something you can influence and control—and on the other departments' capacity to supply crucial data on schedule—something you have no control over.

It is a good idea to have a strategy to coordinate the month-end closure with other departments, remind them of the deadline, and maintain contact, but you also need to have a plan and an accountability agreement in case they don't follow through.

4. Consider your long-term professional goals.
What would be your dream job for the future? What credentials and abilities are required to qualify? Which accomplishments can help you stand out as a qualified and outstanding candidate? Set your professional personal objectives so that you may acquire the necessary knowledge and achievements.

5. Look beyond the present and consider the larger picture.

More important than productivity and skill at your desk is your professional development! A diverse range of abilities and experiences are often needed for career advancement. The capacity to increase your duties and advance in your career depends on your ability to continue learning, so be sure to include professional seminars and other educational opportunities on your list of goals.

Look at rotations in different departments if you want to advance to a VP or C-suite position in the future. Understanding how the many components of the business work together can be helpful and might distinguish you from other applicants.

Finally, Toastmasters is a great approach to hone your public speaking abilities if you envision yourself moving into a management or client-facing capacity.

6. Obtain an understanding of what constitutes objective success.
You are familiar with the fundamentals: A good workplace objective is time-bound, relevant, quantifiable, achievable, and precise. Beyond those fundamentals, consider what it would be like to attain your goals.

Would it facilitate the flow of a certain project? Would it make it possible for the team to collaborate more successfully? You may stay motivated by visualizing a goal you've accomplished.

7. Plan regular check-ins
Setting work objectives involves more than just one meeting at the beginning of the performance period. Any strategy has to be adaptable to be helpful, and professional objectives are no exception. Meet with your

boss to discuss the status and advancement made over the year. These discussions may be formal and scheduled (after each quarter) or more sporadic. Whatever frequency you decide on, it's crucial to maintain contact so that your goal plan may be modified to take into account the realities and priorities of the present.

8. If you need assistance, ask for it.
Star athletes and workers don't have to pull it off by themselves. Additionally, they are aware that having a mentor or coach at their side will enable them to do more and more quickly. You would undoubtedly hire a coach to assist you with your swing if you wanted to grow better at golf. Your career is the same. Find supporters both within and outside of your organization, and create a network of businesspeople who are invested in your success. Talk to them, seek their counsel, and pay close attention.

9. Regularly compare your to-do list with your yearly objectives.

Setting goals at work is a fantastic way to lay out the year's broad objectives and accomplishments. The terrible truth is that it might be challenging to concentrate on the things that everyone had decided were vital because of fire drills and urgent reassignments.

An excellent example is continuing education for professionals. Everyone is aware of its importance for your competence and knowledge. Additionally, many professional qualifications and licenses need to be maintained.

However, due to client expectations, deadlines, and last-minute projects, continuing education so often gets neglected. If you've ever had to finish off a year's worth of schoolwork in the last three weeks of the semester, you're not alone.

So, periodically assess how effectively your daily to-do list corresponds to your overarching professional objectives. Talk to your management and take appropriate action if the two are unrelated.

10. Keep a record of your successes

We've all been there: you're getting ready for your yearly review or updating your résumé for a job hunt when you completely forget about your previous successes. Although your boss is typically pleased with your work and you are aware of how busy you have been, you are unable to remember a single accomplishment during the last year.

The takeaway from this is that it might be difficult to recollect specific success factors after the performance period has ended. You still have a whole year's worth of tasks to consider! Save yourself the hassle and create a simple Word or Excel spreadsheet to keep track of your victories. List everything you've done, from sticking to deadlines to helping out with a last-minute research assignment to delivering persuasive client pitches and presentations.

In conclusion

Keep in mind that it is better to consistently establish objectives for your job. Treat it as an ongoing dialogue as a courtesy to yourself. Request clarification of expectations from your boss for each new task you receive. What do they want your effort to achieve for them? Where do they expect problems to arise? When will this project be completed, and why is it important?

Have a debriefing discussion once the project is over to discuss what went well and what might have been done more effectively. Performance reviews may be intimidating for professionals, but you can only improve if you know what behaviors and abilities require improvement. Maintaining open channels of contact will put you in a position to quickly advance your career and find more exciting jobs.

Chapter 4

Habits to cultivate for efficiency

You may save a lot of time and effort by developing effective working practices. You may reduce procrastination, increase productivity while completing work, enhance communication skills, and generally do your job more efficiently by taking the time to develop new healthy habits.

These healthy habits can also be highly useful to you if you are a remote worker. In my book, **"Remote Work Productivity"**, I extensively highlighted the best approaches in which you can use to maximise your productivity as a remote worker. You should explore the resources contained in that book. It will be of great help to you. However, the guidelines in this chapter will go a long way to help you achieve success.

It only makes sense to use your time at work in a manner that reduces stress and increases productivity.

What are productive working practices?

Both the quality and the efficiency of your job are enhanced by efficient work practices. Effective work habits increase your output while also raising your expectations for how a job or obligation should be carried out. Good work habits are mutually advantageous since they increase job satisfaction. When you perceive that your work is appreciated more, you are inspired to keep performing well. The company is also more successfully achieving its objectives as a result of these productive work habits.

The advantages of productive work practices

As previously noted, productive work habits increase employee happiness and make it easier for the company to achieve its goals. People's professions become more fascinating, less difficult, and more joyful when they have efficient work habits. Additionally, adopting effective work practices can reduce workplace stress and enable people to concentrate more clearly as well as enjoy their professions more. You'll perform better, have more time for learning and growth, be more productive, and manage your time better when you're less stressed. Effective work practices boost employee confidence and help firms achieve their objectives in a highly effective manner.

Here are some tips for developing productive work habits.

1. Utilize the time-blocking strategy

Utilizing the time-blocking strategy is a productive work habit. A time management technique called time blocking is designed to help people divide their workdays into manageable chunks of time. Each block is devoted to doing a certain activity with the idea that the person concentrates only on that task. Time blocking enables you to concentrate on a specific timetable so there is no doubt about what you should prioritize each day and when, as opposed to having an open-ended to-do list. Prepare your work list in advance and be sure to do your weekly evaluation before the next week before setting up your time blocks. In this manner, you are aware of upcoming events, necessary adjustments, and tasks that must be completed.

2. SMART targets

Another strategy for working well is to set SMART objectives. SMART goals are objectives that are simple to specify and carry out. They assist you in determining the tools required to accomplish a task.

Specific, measurable, attainable, pertinent, and time-bound is the acronym for SMART goals.

Your aim should be **specific**, including the intended result and any accompanying expectations.

Measurable: Your objective must be able to be expressed in numbers so that you can monitor your progress. If you want to monitor anything qualitatively, you should figure out how.

Achievable: Your objective must be feasible in light of the resources you currently have at your disposal, and you must be fairly confident in your team's ability to complete it.

Relevant: Your objectives should reflect the ideals of your organization and have a substantial positive effect on your firm.

Your objectives must be **time-bound**, with an expected completion date.

3. Reduce the frequency and length of your meetings.

Limiting the number of meetings you have as well as their length is another strategy to be more productive. Meetings will naturally be shorter and more frequent if you take the effort to plan and conduct more effective meetings than you presently have.

A meeting management technology like Fellow may help you run more planned, thoughtful, and successful meetings. The fellow is remarkable since it combines well with many other tools and technologies thanks to its many extensions, which include a practical Chrome extension. Additionally, Fellow's meeting cost calculator allows you to determine how much it truly costs to get your team together and identify areas where meetings may not be necessary.

4. Use the 80/20 rule to organize your time.

The 80/20 time management strategy, sometimes referred to as Pareto's principle, is an excellent way to develop productive work habits. According to this time-management strategy, just 20% of efforts provide 80% of the outcomes.

Since most workers concentrate on many activities at once rather than concentrating on one crucial activity at a time, this is an excellent strategy to implement if you and your team need to improve your time management abilities. If workers are organized and focused, they can produce 80% of what they need in just 20% of their working hours.

5. Establish and adhere to a system

You may design and adhere to a method to operate more productively. You and your team will be more productive and, therefore, more successful if you establish and adhere to a system. Synchronizing your Google CRM with an accessible integration is an example of a procedure you might include in your daily routine to make work easier.

6. Set and monitor goals

You can be more productive if you set and monitor your goals. Setting goals will become a regular habit that will increase your productivity if done regularly. By precisely documenting, establishing, and monitoring the advancement of your objectives and key outcomes (OKRs) with Fellow's Objectives tool, you can stay on top of your team's goals.

Fellow makes it simple to set new goals, define important outcomes, monitor development, and notify contributors. Each team member can develop their own personal or public OKRs as well as team-wide goals. They just have to go to the My Objectives area. Transparency about corporate objectives may enhance alignment, engagement, and general well-being at work.

These objectives aid workers in understanding the wider picture and how they may contribute. Redesigning the company's identity, for instance, may entail OKRs like developing brand standards, creating a logo, or even organizing a marketing campaign for the next quarter.

7. Teach yourself to say "no"

Saying "no" politely will demonstrate to your colleagues and supervisor that you are not declining work because you don't want to assist them but rather because you are now overburdened and unable to take on extra responsibilities.

Remind yourself that you are useless if you are exhausted, and treat yourself with care. Despite our desire to assist, we must take into account how our response will affect both the asker and ourselves. Never be scared to refuse a request, no matter how modest or large. You will be more efficient and productive at work if you are aware of your boundaries and can effectively convey them.

8. Do not multitask.

Don't multitask as much as you can. Instead of attempting to make progress on numerous tasks at once, concentrate on finishing one job at a time, in order of priority. Ilya Pozin states in a Forbes article on effective habits, "Stop trying to accomplish 10 things at once! Your IQ decreases by an average of 10 points for every task change over a day."

Focusing on one activity at a time can help you do it more quickly and successfully. When it comes to being effective throughout the workplace, less is more. Focus on the fundamentals to increase productivity.

9. Maintain a tidy work area.

This productive work habit seems to be straightforward, and it is. The most crucial benefit of keeping an orderly desk is improved attention. You may focus more clearly and feel less pressured and tempted to engage in activities other than those on your to-do list when your surroundings are tidy and distraction-free. You'll see that you operate more effectively if you appreciate and find your workstation to be nice.

10. Add periodic breaks to your schedule.

Including frequent breaks in your schedule will also increase the productivity of your workday. Overworking often results in additional errors being made, which lowers the quality of your job.

11. Before lunch, concentrate on tough chores.

Finally, give your difficult jobs your full attention early in the day—preferably before lunch. If you take advantage of the fact that most individuals are more alert and focused in the morning, you can postpone your less strenuous and maybe more administrative work until the afternoon.

Furthermore, completing your most difficult chores in the morning will provide you with a strong feeling of inspiration and encouragement, providing you the drive you need to work productively throughout the remainder of the day.

Finally, maximize your productivity by using these 11 effective work habits. Consider using the time-blocking approach, creating SMART objectives, and reducing the number of meetings you and your team have (as well as their length). Think about using the 80/20 rule for time management, developing and sticking to a workable strategy, establishing and monitoring your goals, and developing the ability to say "no" when you're full.

Wherever feasible, refrain from multitasking, keep your workstation tidy and organized, arrange frequent breaks into your daily routine, and concentrate on your most difficult activities before lunch. You'll feel more motivated, pleased, and undoubtedly more productive at work if you adopt these effective work habits.

Chapter 5

Time management techniques for maximum output

Did you know that administrative work takes up to 15 hours a week for microbusinesses with one to nine employees? This is supported by the "Make Business Simple" study from Starling Bank. Even worse, solopreneurs spend 31% of their weekly time organizing their money. Administrative and financial housekeeping is only one of many significant chores that must be completed if you are a company owner or manager, which emphasizes how crucial time management is.

How to be more efficient with your time at work

Planning how to effectively utilize and consciously regulate your time is called time management, and the goal is to increase productivity. Get more done in less time, in essence. Added benefits include:

- improved job standards
- more time to concentrate on strategic or creative tasks less worry
- Reduced procrastination
- more assurance

How to begin going is as follows:

1. Be aware of how you spend your time.
When productivity is calculated based on production over a predetermined time frame, wasted time might translate into lost money. Similar to making a budget, you need to keep track of what you do with your time to identify any activities or routines

that are preventing you from achieving your objectives.

Check the time first. According to the categories you choose, time-tracking software like RescueTime can show you how many hours a day you spend productively compared to how much time you spend on unrelated activities like social media browsing or shopping.

2. Adhere to a daily routine
complete more than just say, "I have eight hours to do XYZ." Make a daily plan with time slots designated for various chores. The secret to success is to stay committed.
Set up realistic timetables. The "planning fallacy," a phenomenon where people overestimate their ability to complete tasks, leads to unduly optimistic delivery forecasts. To ensure that the entire schedule is maintained even if one activity exceeds the

allotted time, include time buffers between them.

Give everything your full attention. Avoid slipping off to websites unrelated to work (or doing anything else you aren't allowed to be doing) during working hours. Close every tab that says "for later" in your browser. Until it's time for a planned break, turn off your phone or put it away. Again, self-control is your greatest friend in this situation.

3. Set priorities.

To-do lists may rescue your productivity. But if you're not cautious, they might grow to such a size and extent that you have no idea where to begin. The Eisenhower Matrix, a tool, may assist you in setting priorities based on significance and urgency. With the use of this decision matrix, you may segment your list into:

- instant action: Important projects with deadlines, or those you put off so long they are past due,
- Set a later date for important projects with no set due date
- Delegate: Tasks that can be performed by others.
- Tasks you may delete since they are not essential to your objectives or purpose

4. Start with the most challenging assignment.

Whether it's a phone call, a favor from a coworker, or that stack of dirty dishes, distractions happen to all of us. Before you know it, the day is passed. The moment has come to "eat that frog."

For those who delay often or have problems avoiding distractions, Brian Tracy's Eat That

Frog productivity technique is effective. It suggests starting with the work that is the largest, trickiest, and most crucial—the one you're most inclined to put off till later. You should only continue once you've "eaten that frog."

5. Process related jobs in batches
Batching, often known as batch processing, is the grouping of related activities for collaborative work. Sort them by purpose or role.

For instance:
Thursday and Wednesday client meetings
Only from 10 to 11 a.m., reply to emails.
early in the morning, produce reports, and disseminate.

6. Establish a suitable time frame

According to Parkinson's law, "Work expands to fill the time allotted to complete it."

You'll probably still take the whole day to finish two jobs that should be completed in only three hours if you had a full day to do so. There's a good possibility you'll still reach the early deadline if you give yourself a shorter time frame.

7. Recognize when to refuse.

Our energy levels are limited each day and decrease with time. Know your limitations and be prepared to say no to prevent doing subpar work. Recognize your advantages and disadvantages. Concentrate on your strengths and, if feasible, delegate tasks that may be completed more quickly and effectively by others.

8. Stop multitasking.

Multitasking reduces productivity and may even be harmful, according to scientists. The American Psychological Association claims that mental juggling has "switching costs" that reduce output. Changing tasks may just take a few seconds each, but if you multitask regularly, it adds up. Your potential for mistakes also increases.

9. Maintain organization.
If any of the following have occurred, you may need an organization makeover:
being late to a meeting you're hosting
You neglected to print a report that your boss required for a presentation.
You repeatedly needed to ask IT for your login or password.

It's excellent news that learning how to be organized is a talent. Start with the fundamentals.

- Keep your work desk tidy. According to National Geographic, psychologists and neuroscientists have linked how clutter affects cognition, mental health, and behavior. Visual clutter may heighten stress and anxiety levels and cause a fight-or-flight reaction.

Get rid of any documents that can be recycled or shredded for improved decision-making. Make room for everyday tools and remove everything unnecessary.

- Organize your shared drives and computer data. When managing digital information, the file name is crucial. Make a system that makes it simple and fast for you and your coworkers to find things.

- Employ a calendar. Put events on your calendar into categories like "personal," "professional," and "commitment." To rapidly distinguish between groups or by urgent vs non-urgent, try using color coding.

10. Employ tools for time management
Use these automation and productivity solutions aimed at increasing productivity:
Slack keeps team interactions in one location that is channel-organized. Getting project specifics no longer requires digging through interminable email conversations.

For storing, sharing, and backing up data, use Dropbox or OneDrive. The files in the cloud are always accessible to authorized team members.

Keeping track of daily, weekly, and monthly schedules is made possible with Google Calendar and Outlook Calendar. To get automated notifications and reminders in the relevant channels, integrate them with Slack.

For designs and diagrams, try Canva and Lucidchart. Even those who struggle with design may use them to build templates that seem polished.

The majority of high-performing teams have mastered the art of time management. Utilize these time management best practices to reclaim your workday, increase productivity, and reduce stress.

Chapter 6

Developing effective communication skills

These days, we communicate with our employees virtually constantly. Saying "hi" to your colleague, having virtual coffee with a distant team member, or sharing a gif of a cat in pajamas with your team may not be thoughtful actions you do, and that's okay. There is a distinction between these kinds of messaging and workplace communication even when you are conversing at work.

When you talk about communicating at work, you're talking about talking about work. Knowing when and how to communicate well at work may help you avoid misunderstandings, improve team morale, boost cooperation, and build trust. Teams that can communicate successfully at work are better equipped to handle challenging circumstances. However, developing effective communication habits requires time and work, which is where we come in.

What exactly is meant by "workplace communication"?

Any kind of communication you have at work about work is considered workplace communication. This covers matters like discussing specific tasks, disseminating project progress updates, and providing managers or staff with feedback. Effective cooperation depends on having good communication skills since poor communication may lead to misunderstandings, misunderstandings, confusion, or even accidentally hurt sentiments.

In the workplace, communication may take place in person, in writing, through video conferencing, or at a group meeting. Additionally, it may take place asynchronously or in real-time while discussing work through email, recorded video, or a platform like a project management application.

Here are some suggestions for improving your ability to communicate at work.

What attributes excellent communication?

How can you begin improving your workplace communication now that you are aware of the types of communication that are permitted? Regardless of the kind of communication, there are a few fundamental principles to follow.

Specifically, effective communication seeks to be clear. Aim to properly explain your point whether you're sending a Slack chat, writing an email, or providing an impromptu response is to prevent conflict rather than to start it. You're contacting to address a concern or encourage productive teamwork on a job or project.

In the workplace, effective communication may highlight obstacles or provide criticism, but make sure the ultimate objective is to improve upon where you are at the moment.

both directions. Even when a person merely communicates nonverbally, every interaction at work involves the exchange of information.

The advantages of open communication in work
In the workplace, good communication can:

- Boost employee commitment and sense of community
- Encourage group commitment
- increasing output
- Create a positive company culture and work environment.
- Conflict reduction and retention

- Advice for improving workplace communication

Where, how, and when you communicate in the workplace are all important factors in effective communication. Try these seven suggestions to improve your communication skills.

1. Be aware of when and where you should communicate.
Face-to-face interactions, emails, instant chats, and platforms for work management are just a few of the various ways that communication takes place. Make sure you're adhering to communication best practices and communicating about the appropriate topics in the right locations for maximum effectiveness.

Sometimes, half the fight is knowing where to communicate. Knowing which communication tool to utilize is crucial since your firm can have a variety of them. Which tool would be best for your inquiry or comment? Should you send an asynchronous message or must you communicate in real time? Ask a teammate or management for advice if you're unsure of the best places to convey such messages. Everyone must agree on everything, and this is crucial. For effective communication, employ:

Slack Asana Gmail Zoom

2. Develop cooperative abilities
The foundation of productive cooperation is collaboration. You must put open and honest communication into practice if you want to develop good team cooperation abilities. This does not always imply constant agreement; teamwork also requires the ability to disagree and resolve conflicts.

Communication and collaboration abilities are rather "chicken and egg" situations. Effective communication is the foundation for excellent cooperation, but collaboration skills are a crucial element of effective communication. In essence, this means that over time, you'll have to practice honing your teamwork and communication abilities. Your ability to communicate ideas and thoughts honestly in a professional setting will increase as your team collaboration skills, which will make cooperation seem more natural.

3. Talk in person whenever you can.
Talking face-to-face is perhaps the most tried-and-true method of preventing misunderstandings. Speaking through video conferencing also works if your team is remote. If you anticipate a difficult talk, face-to-face communication is especially crucial. It might be difficult to convey tone in writing, so it's great if your team member can see your facial expressions and body language.

A phone call might be used as a substitute for a video conference if your team is dispersed or distant. There is such a thing as video conferencing weariness, and it may be especially challenging for distant teams to collaborate and communicate. When you communicate over the phone, you can still hear your team member's voice and tone while reducing some of the visual strain.

4. Pay attention to your tone of voice and body language

It's not only what you say that matters in communication; it's also how you say it. Make sure you are not acting sternly or crossing your arms. Your body language may often have nothing to do with the circumstance; maybe you are exhausted or under stress from your personal life.

However, your team colleagues, who may not be aware of the situation, might see your behavior and infer that you are disturbed or furious. Try to relax your body language and facial emotions, especially during difficult talks, to prevent unintentionally sending the wrong signals.

5. Give two-way communication a top priority.
In the workplace, listening is just as crucial to communication as talking. Listening to others' ideas rather than just attempting to share your own is a crucial component of working collaboratively with others.

Listening to respond and listening to comprehend are the two most prevalent styles of listening. When you listen to respond, you aren't listening to what the other person is saying; rather, you are thinking about what you are going to say next. When you listen in this way, you run the danger of missing important details or even repeating what the other person just said.

Instead, make an effort to "listen to understand," which means to pay attention to what the other person is saying without formulating a response. If you do have anything to say, write it down so you can return to listening to comprehend rather than focusing on attempting to recall what you want to say next.

6. Remain factual and avoid fiction.
The method "Facts vs. stories" is one that Diana Chapman, the co-founder of the Conscious Leadership Group, suggests. The "facts" in this situation are things that really occurred and on which everyone in the room might readily agree. A "story," on the other hand, is how you choose to see the circumstance.

Say, for example, that during a brief team meeting, your boss offers you real-time feedback. It is true that. The criticism caught you off guard, and you believe that your boss shared it with you rather than reserving it for your 1:1 because they were unhappy with your job. This is a "story" since there is no way for you to verify whether it is real or not.

Stories are unavoidable; we all construct them using facts. But make an effort to distinguish between tales and facts, and hold off on acting on stories until you can verify them. For instance, you could want to question your boss why they provided comments at a team meeting during your next 1:1 meeting.

7. Verify you are chatting with the appropriate individual.
Both who you're talking to and what you say matter in effective professional communication. When you communicate to the wrong individuals or attempt to impart knowledge in the incorrect situation, poor communication often results.

Make sure the appropriate individuals are in the room or are getting the message to prevent this. Go through an activity to find any significant project stakeholders that could be absent if you are unsure of who that would be.

Lastly
Having a single source of truth for all of your communications and work-related information is the last element of clear communication. You may assist your team in coordinating work at all levels by using a centralized system, such as a task management application.

Chapter 7

Improving decision-making and problem-solving

We encounter many issues in life that call for us to make choices. While some are minor and easily fixed, others may be more and more involved. But what if you could become an expert at making decisions and solving problems?

We will go into great detail on problem-solving and decision-making in this chapter, as well as their significance and the science underlying them. Additionally, we will provide you with tried-and-true methods for solving issues and making wise judgments.

In this extensive chapter on mastering the art of problem-solving and decision-making, we have everything covered. So grab a seat as we lead you on an educational trip to master problem-solving!

Understanding decision-making and problem-solving

Although the terms problem-solving and decision-making are often used interchangeably, they are not the same. Here is a quick breakdown of how issue-solving and decision-making differ: solving issues Identification, analysis, and resolution of problems or issues constitute problem-solving. It entails identifying the underlying source of an issue and coming up with methods to solve it.

Critical thinking, inventiveness, and analytical abilities are necessary for problem resolution. It is a method that may address both straightforward and intricate issues in a variety of situations, including social, business, and organizational ones. Making decisions Making decisions involves selecting a path of action from a range of options. It entails weighing the pros and drawbacks of several possibilities and choosing the optimal course of action in light of the information and standards at hand.

Critical thinking, judgment, and assessment abilities are necessary for decision-making. It is a method that may be used to basic and difficult choices in a variety of situations, including organizational, professional, and personal ones.

Why are decision-making and problem-solving abilities crucial in the workplace?

Decision-making and problem-solving abilities are crucial in the workplace for several reasons.
Efficiency and productivity are increased because employees with good problem-solving and decision-making

abilities are better able to recognize and address potential challenges at work. As a result, they are more productive and efficient since they can finish their task more quickly.

Enhanced customer satisfaction: Employees that are adept at problem-solving and making decisions are better able to allay the worries and grievances of any possible clients. Customers believe their requirements are being met and their issues are being handled, which increases customer happiness.

Effective collaboration Problem-solving and decision-making abilities are necessary for productive teamwork while working in groups. Groups with better problem-solving skills have a higher chance of succeeding in their objectives.
Problem-solving and decision-making abilities are also essential for fostering creativity at work. Employees that use their

imagination to solve issues are more likely to come up with novel solutions that will advance the company.

Risk management: The ability to solve problems and make decisions is also essential for managing risk in the workplace. Employees may lessen risks' detrimental effects on the company by detecting possible risks and creating ways to reduce them.

Overall, decision-making and problem-solving abilities are crucial in the workplace because they enable workers to recognize issues and find solutions, collaborate well in teams, promote creativity, and control risk. Employers strongly respect these talents since they are necessary for a company to succeed.

Five Methods for Problem-Solving Success

Here are five alternative problem-solving methods and tactics, each with a practical application example:

Brainstorming: Brainstorming is a method for coming up with original ideas and challenges to solve. People discuss ideas and build on one another's proposals during a brainstorming session. The objective is to quickly produce a huge number of ideas. For instance, a group of engineers may utilize brainstorming to generate fresh ideas for enhancing the effectiveness of a production process.

Root Cause Analysis: Locating a problem's root cause is a strategy used in root cause analysis. To find the source of the issue, "why" inquiries must be asked. Actions may be performed to address the underlying cause when it has been found. For instance, a hospital may employ root cause analysis to look into the reasons behind patient falls and pinpoint the main culprits, such as insufficient personnel or bad lighting.

SWOT analysis is a method for assessing the advantages, disadvantages, strengths, and threats associated with a scenario or issue. It entails evaluating internal and external elements that might have an influence on the issue and figuring out how to take advantage of strengths and opportunities while reducing weaknesses and threats. A small firm, for instance, may use SWOT analysis to assess its position in the market and find chances to broaden its product offering or boost its marketing.

Pareto analysis is a method for determining the most important issues to deal with. It entails prioritizing the most important problems and rating problems based on their importance and frequency. A software development team, for instance, may use Pareto analysis to rank defects and other problems in order of importance to the user experience.

Using a decision matrix, you may compare your options and decide which course of action is best. To compare alternatives based on criteria and weighted factors, a matrix must be created. The option with the highest score is then chosen. A manager may, for instance, use decision matrix analysis to compare several software providers based on factors like pricing, features, and support before choosing the vendor with the highest overall score.

Five Methods for Making Good Decisions

Here are five alternative methods and approaches for making decisions, each with a sample application:

Cost-Benefit Evaluation Cost-benefit analysis is a method for weighing the advantages and disadvantages of various solutions. The predicted costs and advantages of each alternative are compared, and the one with the greatest net benefit is chosen. For instance, a business may assess the potential ROI of a new product line using cost-benefit analysis.

Decision Trees: A visual depiction of the decision-making process is a decision tree. They include outlining prospective outcomes and probability for various possibilities. Taking into account the possibility of various outcomes, this aids in determining the optimal course of action. A farmer, for instance, may use a decision tree to choose the crops to grow following the predicted weather patterns.

SWOT analysis is a tool that may be used to make decisions. A decision maker may assess the possible risks and rewards of each choice by determining its strengths, weaknesses, opportunities, and threats. A company owner may, for instance, utilize SWOT analysis to weigh the advantages and possible dangers of entering a new market.

The benefits and drawbacks of various solutions are listed in a pros and cons study. Choosing the optimal course of action includes assessing the advantages and disadvantages of each choice. A person may utilize a pros and cons analysis, for instance, to determine whether to accept a job offer.

Six hats for thinking: The six thinking hats method helps you consider an issue from several angles. Six distinct "hats" are used to examine various decision-related factors. White represents facts and numbers, red represents emotions and sentiments, black represents dangers and disadvantages, yellow represents opportunities and rewards, green represents innovation and fresh ideas, and blue represents overview and control.

For instance, a team may assess many ideas for a marketing campaign using the six-thinking hats approach.

These methods and approaches may be beneficial for making decisions in various circumstances. A decision maker, for instance, may examine possibilities more objectively and make better decisions by employing a systematic approach to decision-making.

Conclusion
The ability to solve problems and make decisions effectively is crucial for both personal and professional success. It enables you to swiftly accomplish your objectives, solve challenging challenges, and make well-informed judgments. You may improve your ability to solve problems and make decisions by properly using these 10 strategies, which will also help you become a more effective and successful person.

Therefore, begin using these strategies right now to get toward your objectives.

Highly productive individuals might seem to be robots or magicians. Most of the time, the most effective individuals you encounter have discovered strategies for overcoming obstacles like procrastination.

Our four primary productivity suggestions are summarized here. How to be more productive is as follows:

- Time management is key.
- Improve your to-do lists.
- Taking good care of yourself
- Finally, know when to seek assistance.

Smart individuals seek assistance. Productive people are honest about their ignorance. Asking for assistance rather than attempting to figure anything out on your own can save you time (and stress). Make sure you are aware of your resources, who and what they are, and develop the practice of asking for assistance.

www.ingramcontent.com/pod-product-compliance
Lightning Source LLC
Chambersburg PA
CBHW062354290526
45794CB00005B/2214